The Oxford Piano Method

Piano Time Sports

Book 1

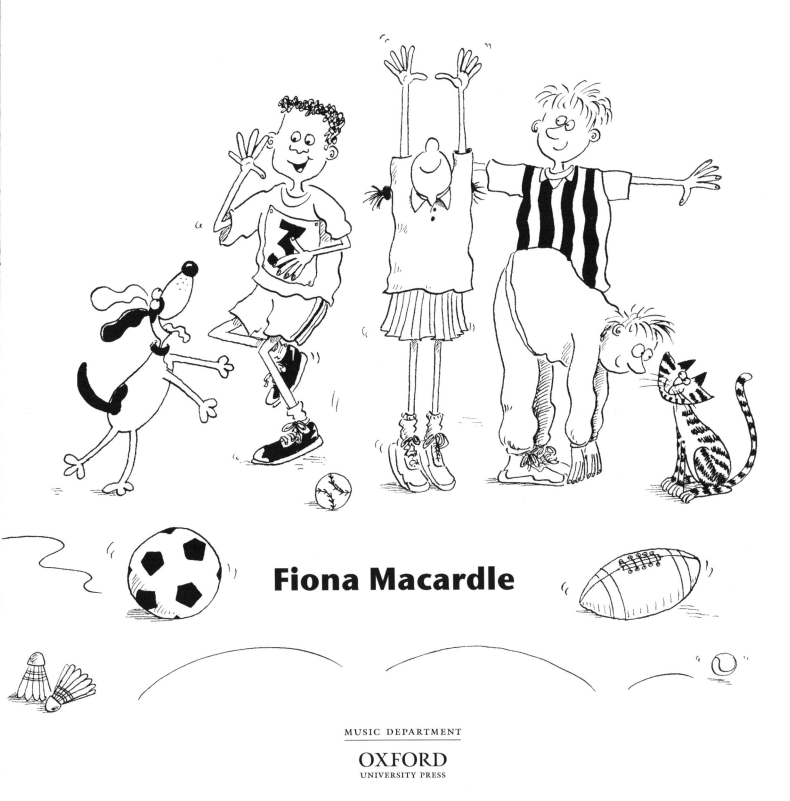

Fiona Macardle

MUSIC DEPARTMENT

OXFORD
UNIVERSITY PRESS

OXFORD
UNIVERSITY PRESS

Great Clarendon Street, Oxford OX2 6DP, England
198 Madison Avenue, New York, NY10016, USA

Oxford University Press is a department of the University of Oxford.
It furthers the University's aim of excellence in research, scholarship,
and education by publishing worldwide

Oxford is a registered trade mark of Oxford University Press
in the UK and in certain other countries

21

ISBN 978-0-19-372773-1

Music and text origination by
Barnes Music Engraving Ltd., East Sussex
Printed in Great Britain on acid-free paper by
Halstan & Co. Ltd., Amersham, Bucks.

With many thanks to my own teachers:
Josephine O'Carroll
Fintan O'Carroll
Eric de Courcy
Margaret Bowden

Piano Time Sports

When we learn a new sport, we take it for granted that we will need to do warming up exercises. Learning the piano is no different. Just as in any sporting activity, a few technical exercises can increase control, reduce muscle stress, and prevent strain. This book introduces essential workouts for the hands in a gradual and fun way. Make these activities a regular part of lesson and practice time. Pick one or two each time you practise and use them to warm up.

There are 10 sessions, each focusing on a particular technical point. Each session contains:

- **Warm ups:** first, a very simple workout of a bar or two for repetition, so that you can concentrate on the technique rather than the notes. Try hands separately and together. Try them in different keys and in different octaves on the piano. Try playing them with different dynamics. 'Coach's tip' helps you get the best out of these. Second, a warm up, also based on the technique, for the piece on the opposite page.

- **Midweek training:** a short, simple piece practising the new technique.

- **Fitness level:** a more extended piece, also based on the technique, and designed to show off your new-found skill!

Contents

Session 1: *Just for starters—simple 5-finger exercises*

Warm ups

Here are some simple tips to get you into gear for a really good practice session:

1. Rub your hands together and make sure they are warm.
2. Wring your hands; imagine you are putting on lots of cream.
3. Link your fingers and push your hands as far forward as you can.
4. Push your shoulders right up to your ears and squeeze. Let go, then roll your shoulders forwards and then backwards.
5. Now sit comfortably on your piano stool, making sure you are the correct distance from the piano and that your feet are in the right position (if you are big enough to reach the floor!). Your teacher will be able to help you check this.

> **Coach's tip:** Athletes wear tracksuits when training. This keeps their muscles warm, especially when working in the cold. Piano playing is very similar, so keep your hands warm—wear gloves beforehand if you are going to practise in a cold room.

Midweek training: *Onto the field*

Running on the spot

Three-legged race

Make sure the notes go down at exactly the same time.

Session 2: *Legato (smoothly)*

Warm ups

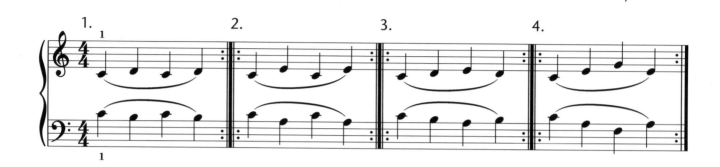

Coach's tip: Choose and play one bar, one hand at a time, making sure there are no gaps between the notes. Now try hands together. Keep your wrist just above the level of the keys and your arm relaxed.

Warm up for **Cross-country skiing**

Midweek training: *Slalom*

Lift your hand at the end of each phrase.

Cross-country skiing

At a good pace

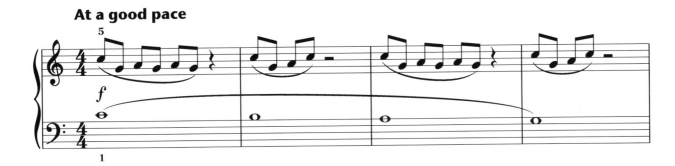

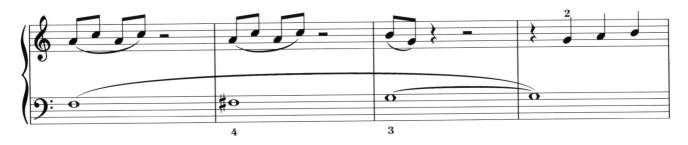

Session 3: *Staccato (detached)*

Warm ups

> **Coach's tip:** Relax your hands between each staccato note. This means that you have to start quite slowly so you can feel the difference. Stay close to the keys with a quick finger movement. Try hands separately and together, and try the warm ups in different keys.

Warm up for **Taking the penalty**

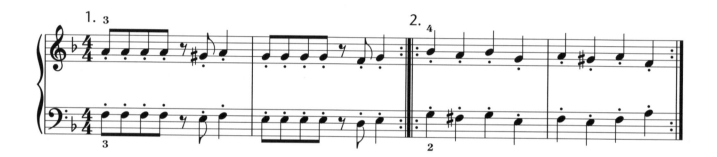

Midweek training: *Dribbling the ball*

Taking the penalty

Steady

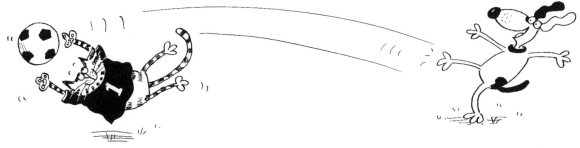

Session 4: *The down-up movement*

Warm ups

> **Coach's tip:** Imagine you are a puppet with the string attached above your wrist. Lower the wrist as you play the first note and raise it as you lift your hand off at the end of each bar.

Warm up for **Testing the trampoline**

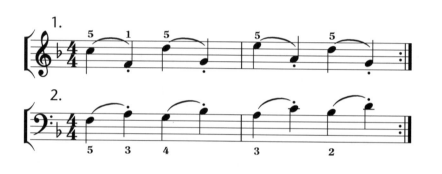

Midweek training: *Springboard*

Testing the trampoline

Lightly and with bounce!

Session 5: *Gentle wrist rotation*

Warm ups

Coach's tip: *Imagine you are rocking your hand very slightly. Only go as far as your hand will stretch.*

Now hands together – slowly!

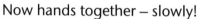

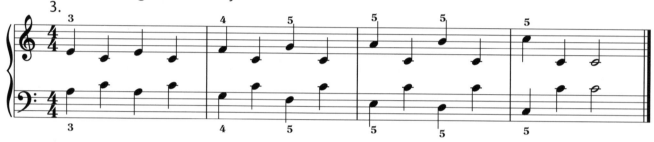

Warm up for **Golf swing**

Midweek training: *Pitch and putt*

Confident

Golf swing

Swing the rhythm and play with a jaunty feel.

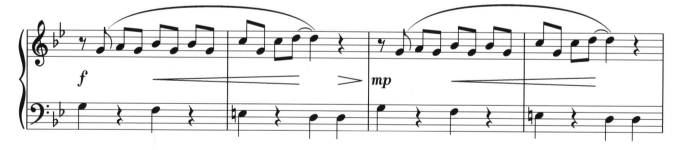

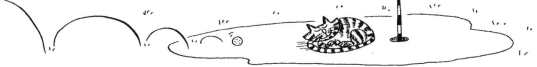

Session 6: *Chords*

Warm ups

Coach's tip: Be careful to get both notes down at exactly the same time.

1.

2.

3.

4.

Warm up for **Tap dance**

Midweek training: *Slow toe tap*

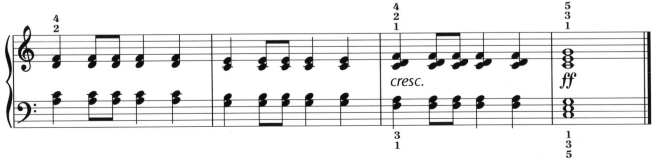

14

Tap dance

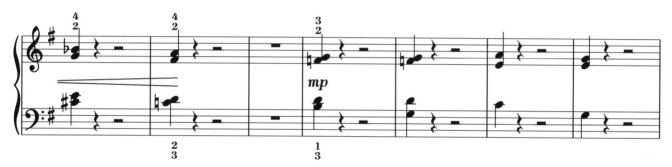

Session 7: *Strengthening weak fingers*

Warm ups

> **Coach's tip:** Lift the middle joints of your fingers high. Keep the fingers and hand rounded and over the keys, particularly when using 4th and 5th fingers.

Warm up for **Cross-Channel swim**

Midweek training: *Treading water*

Cross-Channel swim

With a steady pace

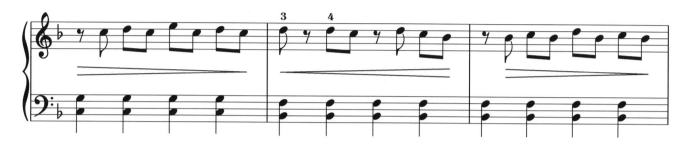

Warm ups

> **Coach's tip:** Take this slowly at first. Keep your hand light and don't 'push' into the keys. If it feels uncomfortable as you get quicker, stop and rest your hand on your knee.

Warm up for **Gymnastic display**

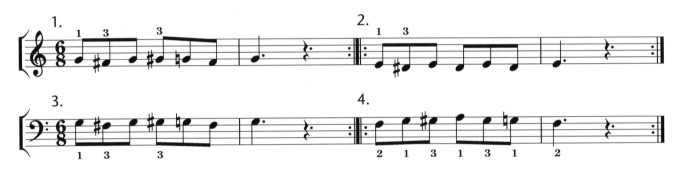

Midweek training: *On the beam*

18

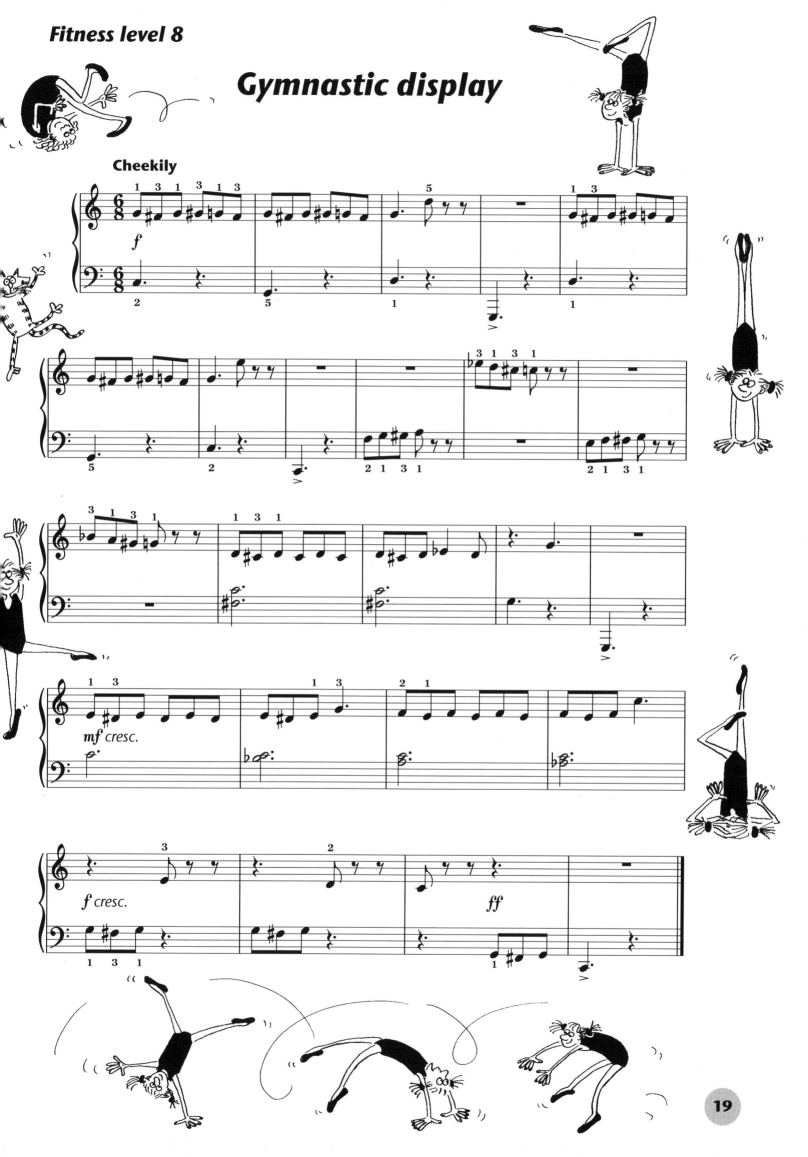

Session 9: *Hand-crossing*

Warm ups

> Coach's tip: Keep the moving hand relaxed, and think in one 'sweep' up and down the keys.

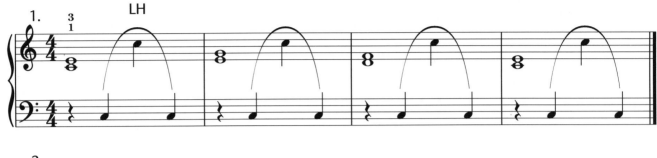

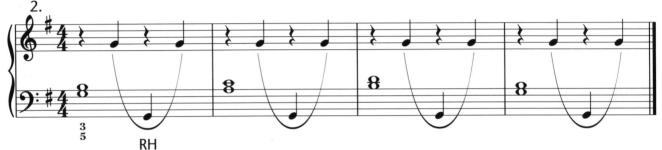

Warm up for **Beating the opposition**

Midweek training: *Limbering up*

Join each phrase smoothly between the hands.

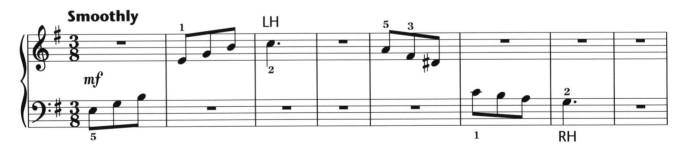

Beating the opposition

With confidence

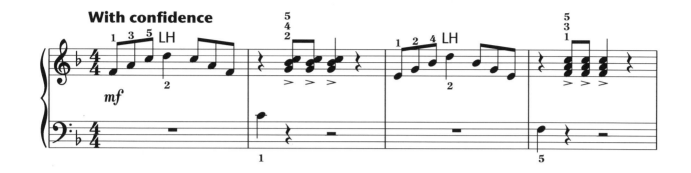

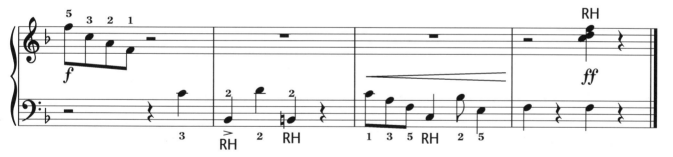

Session 10: Scales up to scratch!

Congratulations! You've kept up with your training all the way, so in this session there are *two* pieces in which you can demonstrate your fitness level!

Warm ups

> **Coach's tip:** *Try these hands together and separately. Keep your hands slightly turned towards your thumb at all times—it's then much easier to reach under to the next note.*

Warm up for **Victory parade** (see page 24)

Put your thumb down smoothly as you turn.

Midweek training: *Hook, line and sinker*

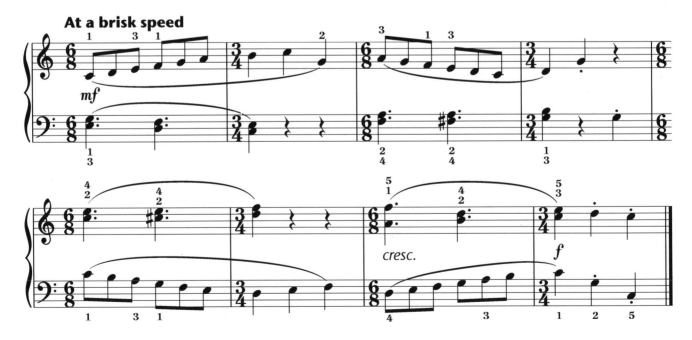

22

Just fishin'

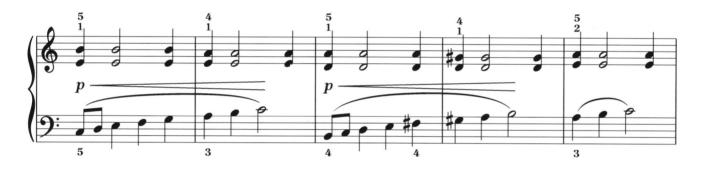

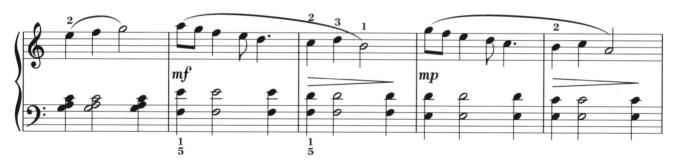

Victory parade

Briskly

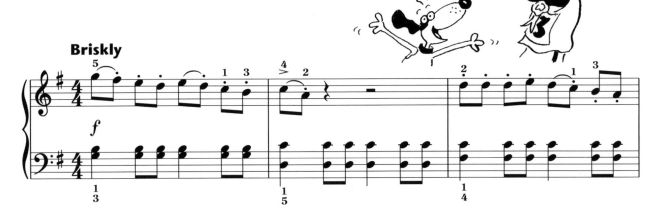

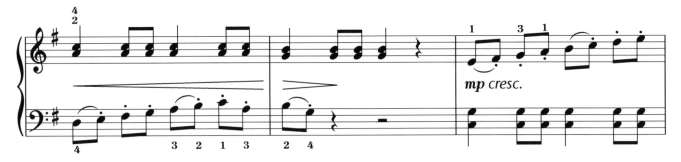